978-1-967192-52-6 paperback

Table of Contents

"The art and essence of ministry" refers to the multifaceted nature of serving others, particularly in a religious or community context.

Art: This implies that ministry involves creativity, skill, and personal expression. It encompasses the ability to communicate, inspire, and connect with people on a deeper level. The practice of ministry is not just about following a set of rules or traditions; it requires intuition and adaptability to meet the unique needs of individuals and communities.

Essence: This aspect focuses on the core values and principles that underpin ministry. It includes compassion, empathy, service, and a commitment to the well-being of others. The essence of ministry is about fostering relationships, nurturing spiritual growth, and embodying the teachings and values one represents.

Together, the art and essence of ministry highlight the importance of both the skills involved and the fundamental principles that guide a minister's work, emphasizing the need for both heart and technique in serving others effectively.

Acknowledgments

I want to extend my heartfelt thanks to everyone who played a role in bringing "The Art and Essence of Ministry" to life. First and foremost, I give my gratitude to God the Father, God the Son, and God the Holy Spirit! I am especially thankful to my teacher, Dr. Kerry Williams of Sunset International Bible Institute, whose wisdom and guidance have been invaluable throughout this journey. Your insights into the nuances of ministry have profoundly shaped my understanding and passion for this vocation.

I am also deeply appreciative of my colleagues in ministry, Gerry Binford, Stanley Boyd, and Anthony Jernagin, who generously shared their experiences and perspectives, enriching the content of this book. Your stories have inspired me and highlighted the significant impact of our work.

A heartfelt thank you to my wife, Michelle, of 32 years, who has been my rock, encouraging and supporting me through sleepless nights, prayer, and the shared joys and challenges of my ministry. To my sons, Sherif and Desean, your unwavering support means the world to me. I also want to acknowledge my father and mother-in-law, Alma and the late Albert Curtis, whose belief in me has been a constant source of strength.

I would like to recognize the many individuals I've encountered throughout my ministry. Each of you has imparted something invaluable, contributing to the art and essence of serving. Special thanks to Dr. Harvey M. Jackson, my father in the gospel; Jack King, who taught me the gospel; Minister Walter Williams, under whom I served for some time; my high school English teacher, Frances Isaac; Linda and the late George Smith Sr.; Jerry and Ann Minor; Patty and the late Sid Smith; Dr. Gary Bradley; Jason Bybee; Lee Milan; Dick Savage; the Mayfair Church of Christ; and many others.

Finally, I dedicate this book to my mother, the late Sammie Jean Smith, my brother, the late Robert Lee Smith Jr., and the Lakewood Church of Christ in Huntsville, AL.

Thank you all for being a part of this journey.

Introduction

At its core, Christian ministry is the act of serving others and spreading the message of Jesus Christ. It involves living out one's faith through actions that demonstrate love, compassion, and service to those in need. Christian ministry can take many forms, from leading a congregation to volunteering at a local charity, but the ultimate goal is always to glorify God and share His love with the world.

Being involved in ministry signifies a commitment to being a faithful follower of Jesus. Disciples engaged in ministry not only deepen their own faith but also foster the growth of others. They achieve this by:

- Building meaningful relationships

- Leading by example

- Teaching biblical truths

- Encouraging spiritual disciplines

- Providing practical guidance

- Empowering others to serve

- Fostering accountability

- Multiplying disciples

Ministry often encompasses discipleship, which involves teaching and training others in both biblical and practical theology. This can occur in formal settings through Scripture study or informally through modeling behavior.

The ultimate aim of discipleship is to cultivate mature believers who can, in turn, disciple others. This mission aligns with the Great Commission, as articulated by Jesus in Matthew 28:19-20: "Go therefore and make disciples of all nations, baptizing them in the name of the Father and of the Son and of the Holy Spirit, teaching them to observe all that I have commanded you. And behold, I am with you always, to the end of the age (ESV)."

Ministry involves a vibrant community dedicated to fostering spiritual growth, connection, and service. It takes the power of faith to transform lives and bring people together. Ministries provide guidance, support, and encouragement as everyone navigates life's challenges and joys. Through worship, education, and outreach, the ministry aims to create an inclusive environment where everyone feels valued and empowered. Ministry, at its core, is about serving others and fostering spiritual growth and community well-being. While commonly associated with religious institutions, the principles of ministry extend to various fields, including social work, education, mental health, and community organizing. This paper seeks to elucidate the art of ministry, how it is practiced creatively and effectively, and its essence, which is deeply tied to compassion, leadership, and transformation. Join me as we explore my beliefs, engage with one another, and make a positive impact in our world. Together, we can deepen our faith and inspire change within ourselves and our communities through ministry.

This book examines the interplay between the art and essence of spiritual ministry, with a focus on how creative practices foster spiritual growth and community connection. It posits that spiritual ministry is not solely an administrative or doctrinal conversation function but a dynamic art form that involves the holistic engagement of individuals in their spiritual journeys. By analyzing the roles of ritual, music, visual arts, and storytelling in spiritual ministry, the study explores how these artistic elements foster deeper connections with the divine and with one another. Through case studies and interviews with spiritual leaders and practitioners, the research highlights the transformative power of integrating artistic expression into spiritual practices, ultimately arguing that such integration can lead to enriched spiritual experiences, increased community cohesion, and broader social impact. This book aims to offer a new framework for understanding spiritual ministry as an evolving art that responds to the needs of contemporary society.

Ministry, whether in a religious or governmental context, comes with its own set of advantages and disadvantages. There are pros and cons in ministry. A person must be willing to sacrifice and live within the will of God to enhance and produce effective ministry. Here are some pros and cons to consider:

Pros

1. Purpose and Fulfillment: Many people find deep satisfaction and meaning in serving others and contributing to a greater cause.

2. Community Engagement: Ministry often involves active participation in community building, fostering connections and support networks.

3. Leadership Development: It provides opportunities to develop leadership skills and influence positive change.

4. Spiritual Growth: It can lead to personal spiritual development and a deeper understanding of faith. It will increase your faith in God and build a personal relationship with Christ as you seek him for guidance.

5. Support Systems: Ministries often create strong support systems for individuals in need, offering assistance and guidance.

Cons

1. Emotional Toll: The responsibilities can be emotionally draining, especially when dealing with crises or community issues.

2. Burnout Risk: High demands and expectations can lead to burnout and fatigue among those in ministry roles.

3. Financial Constraints: Many ministries operate on limited budgets, which can restrict resources and funding for projects.

4. Conflict and Criticism: Ministers may face conflict within their communities and criticism from those who disagree with their views or methods.

5. Work-Life Balance: The nature of ministry can blur the lines between personal and professional life, making it difficult to maintain a healthy balance.

Each person's experience in ministry can vary greatly based on their context, role, and personal resilience. The art and essence of ministry lie in the delicate balance between compassionate service and transformative leadership, where the minister not only imparts spiritual and moral guidance but also fosters community resilience and personal growth, ultimately creating a holistic environment that nurtures the well-being of individuals and the collective."

This book explores the multifaceted nature of ministry, emphasizing its role in shaping lives and communities through a blend of empathy, ethical principles, and proactive engagement.

Historical Context of Ministry

The concept of ministry has evolved over centuries, influenced by cultural, social, and theological shifts. In ancient times, ministry was often performed by priests and spiritual leaders tasked with mediating between the divine and the community. The rise of various religious movements brought new interpretations and practices of ministry, emphasizing personal connection and community involvement. This section will explore key historical developments and their implications for contemporary ministry.

The history of ministry is rich and varied, tracing its roots back to the earliest days of religious practice and community leadership.

Ancient Origins

Ministry can be seen as a response to humanity's desire for spiritual guidance and connection. In ancient civilizations, religious leaders, such as priests and shamans, played crucial roles in mediating between the divine and the community. These figures often conducted rituals, offered sacrifices, and provided counsel based on their understanding of spiritual matters.

The Early Church

The concept of ministry took on a more formal structure with the emergence of Christianity in the 1st century AD. Jesus Christ appointed disciples to spread his teachings, and after his resurrection, they became the early leaders of the Christian community. The apostles, particularly Peter and Paul, traveled extensively to establish churches and guide believers, emphasizing the importance of teaching, prayer, and communal support.

Development of Church Hierarchies

As Christianity spread throughout the Roman Empire, the need for organized leadership became apparent. By the 2nd and 3rd centuries, various roles, including those of bishops, deacons, and presbyters, emerged, each with distinct functions in the ministry. This hierarchical structure was formalized over the centuries, culminating in the establishment of the Catholic Church, which further defined the roles and responsibilities of its ministry.

Reformation and New Perspectives

The Protestant Reformation in the 16th century introduced significant changes to ministry. Reformers such as Martin Luther and John Calvin challenged the existing ecclesiastical hierarchy and emphasized the concept of the priesthood of all believers. This shift encouraged lay participation in ministry, promoting the idea that all Christians are called to serve and share their faith.

Modern Developments

In the 19th and 20th centuries, ministry continued to evolve, influenced by social changes and the rise of new denominations. Movements such as Methodism, Pentecostalism, and the Social Gospel emphasized different aspects of ministry, including personal holiness, spiritual gifts, and social justice.

Contemporary Ministry

Today, ministry encompasses a wide range of expressions across various Christian traditions. It includes not only preaching and teaching but also community service, counseling, and advocacy. The rise of technology and digital communication has further expanded the ways in which ministry can be conducted, allowing for innovative approaches to outreach and discipleship.

Throughout its history, the ministry has remained rooted in the call to serve God and others, adapting to meet the spiritual and practical needs of communities across cultures and eras.

The Art of Ministry

The art of ministry from a spiritual perspective transcends mere organizational structures and frameworks; it involves a deep, transformative engagement with the divine and the community. This art is rooted in a profound understanding of spiritual principles, relational dynamics, and the call to serve others with love and compassion.

1. Spiritual Calling and Identity

At the heart of ministry lies a sense of calling. Those engaged in ministry often feel a divine prompting or vocation to serve, which shapes their identity and purpose. This calling is not just about fulfilling duties but about embodying the love and teachings of Jesus Christ. It requires a continual process of spiritual formation, where ministers cultivate their relationship with God through prayer, study, and reflection.

2. Relationship Building

Ministry is inherently relational. The art of ministry involves building authentic connections with individuals and communities. This means listening deeply, empathizing with others' struggles, and celebrating their joys. Effective ministers create spaces for vulnerability and trust, allowing people to encounter God's love through their interactions. Relationships are nurtured through shared experiences, whether in worship, service, or fellowship.

3. Spiritual Guidance and Discernment

A significant aspect of ministry is providing spiritual guidance. This requires discernment, an ability to seek God's will in various situations and help others do the same. Ministers often act as spiritual companions, helping individuals navigate their faith journeys, confront challenges, and recognize God's presence in their lives. This guidance is steeped in prayer, scripture, and a deep understanding of spiritual principles.

4. Teaching and Discipleship

The art of ministry also includes teaching biblical truths and fostering discipleship. This involves not only imparting knowledge but also modeling what it means to live out one's faith. Effective teaching inspires others to explore their spirituality, encouraging them to develop their own relationship with God. Discipleship is a lifelong journey, inviting individuals to grow and mature in their faith while equipping them to disciple others.

5. Service and Compassion

Ministry is an expression of service rooted in Christ's example of humility and compassion. The art of ministry involves recognizing the needs of others and responding with grace and action. Whether through outreach, advocacy, or community service, ministers embody the call to love one's neighbor. This service is an outpouring of genuine concern for others, reflecting God's love in tangible ways.

6. Spiritual Practices

The art of ministry is also enriched by spiritual practices that nurture personal and communal faith. Prayer, worship, fasting, and meditation are vital components that draw individuals closer to God and strengthen their ministry. These practices create a rhythm of spiritual life that sustains ministers and their communities, fostering a deeper awareness of God's presence and action.

7. Empowerment and Multiplication

Finally, effective ministry seeks to empower others to serve within their own contexts. This involves recognizing and nurturing the gifts and callings of individuals, encouraging them to take on roles of leadership and service. By fostering an environment where others can thrive, ministers participate in the multiplication of disciples, fulfilling the Great Commission.

In summary, the art of ministry from a spiritual perspective is a holistic endeavor that integrates calling, relationship, guidance, teaching, service, spiritual practices, and empowerment. It requires a deep commitment to both personal and communal growth in faith, aimed at creating a transformative impact in the lives of individuals and the broader community.

Creative Expression in Ministry

Ministry can be viewed as a form of art where practitioners engage in creative expression to connect with individuals and communities. This section examines various artistic elements of ministry, including:

Storytelling: The power of narratives in conveying spiritual truths and fostering connection. **Music/Singing and Worship**: The role of singing in enhancing worship experiences and community engagement.

Visual Arts: How art installations and visual expressions can provoke thought and inspire faith.

Storytelling is a powerful tool in the art and essence of ministry, serving as a means to communicate profound truths, foster connection, and inspire transformation. Its effectiveness lies in several key aspects:

1. Relatability and Connection

Stories have the unique ability to resonate with people on a personal level. They draw listeners in by reflecting on shared experiences, emotions, and challenges. In ministry, sharing personal anecdotes or biblical narratives helps congregants see themselves in the story, making spiritual teachings more relatable and accessible. This connection fosters a sense of community and belonging, as individuals recognize that they are not alone in their journeys.

2. Engaging the Imagination

Stories engage the imagination, inviting listeners to visualize and emotionally connect with the narrative. This engagement can enhance understanding and retention of spiritual truths. When a minister shares a compelling story, it captures the audience's attention, allowing them to ponder the deeper meanings and implications long after the message has been delivered.

3. Conveying Complex Truths

Many spiritual concepts can be abstract or difficult to grasp. Storytelling simplifies these complexities by illustrating them through relatable scenarios. For example, parables used by Jesus, such as the Good Samaritan or the Prodigal Son, distill profound moral and theological lessons into memorable narratives. This method helps individuals internalize and apply biblical teachings in their own lives.

4. Inspiring Action and Transformation

Effective stories often include elements of conflict, resolution, and transformation. When listeners witness the journeys of characters—whether real or fictional—they are inspired to reflect on their own lives and consider how they might respond to similar situations. Stories of faith, redemption, and perseverance encourage individuals to take action, whether that means deepening their faith, serving others, or making positive changes in their lives.

5. Preserving Tradition and Community Identity

Storytelling is a way to preserve the history and traditions of a faith community. By sharing stories of past leaders, significant events, and personal testimonies, ministers help to create a collective identity that strengthens community bonds. These narratives not only honor the past but also inspire future generations to carry on the values and beliefs of their faith.

6. Facilitating Spiritual Reflection

Stories can serve as a catalyst for reflection and discussion. When a minister shares a story, it often prompts questions, dialogue, and a deeper exploration of faith. This reflective process encourages congregants to consider their beliefs, values, and spiritual practices, fostering a culture of growth and inquiry within the community.

7. Enhancing Worship Experiences

Incorporating storytelling into worship services can enrich the overall experience. Whether through testimonies, dramatic readings, or multimedia presentations, stories can complement singing, prayer, and teaching, creating a more dynamic and immersive worship environment. This integration helps to convey the essence of faith in a way that is both engaging and meaningful.

In conclusion, storytelling is an essential aspect of ministry that enhances communication, fosters connection and inspires transformation. By weaving narratives into the fabric of ministry, leaders can effectively convey spiritual truths, engage their communities, and cultivate a deeper understanding of faith. Storytelling not only enriches the ministerial experience but also empowers individuals to embrace their own stories as part of the greater narrative of God's love and grace.

Skills and Techniques

Effective ministry requires a range of skills, including emotional intelligence, communication, and conflict resolution. This section will analyze the techniques used by successful ministers to create meaningful interactions, build trust, and facilitate healing and growth.

[1]In Dr. O.J. Shabazz's book Excellence in Ministry, he explains how teaching and preaching are one of the highest calling in the

---

[1] Shabazz, Dr. O.J., Excellence in Ministry (Orlando: ISBN: 979-8-218-23336-5, 2023)

land. It is difficult to determine the proper place to employ ministry. First and foremost, how does a minister determine the best place for ministry? [2]The Bible teaches in Matthew 28:19-20: Jesus said therefore, go and make disciples of all nations, baptizing them in the name of the Father and of the Son and of the Holy Spirit, **20** and teaching them to obey everything I have commanded you. And surely, I am with you always, to the very end of the age (NIV)." This teaches that the need for ministry is everywhere. Souls exist everywhere in this world therefore, ministry should be throughout this world as well. Ministry meets the needs of individuals to draw them to Christ. Dr. Shabazz gives several developments within his book where ministers may fit best to use their talents and gifts to the best of their abilities for the upbuilding of the kingdom. All who have been baptized into Christ have been called to his ministry.

Many ministers aspire to serve in large congregations. However, rural congregations, often consisting of only a handful of people, also require pastoral care. As churches in rural areas grow more diverse, opportunities arise for ministers to engage in these communities. Additionally, congregations are becoming increasingly racially diverse, highlighting the critical need to build trust and foster interactions among all members. Unfortunately, many of our young, energetic parishioners are graduating and leaving for better opportunities, making rural ministry less appealing.

[3]Here are some common reasons people may hesitate or leave rural ministry:

- Isolation from family and friends

---

[2] Holman, Rainbow Study Bible (Nashville: Holman Bible Publishers, 2015)
[3] Lean, Murray, The Joys (and Challenges) of Rural Ministry (2019) https://au.thegospelcoalition.org/article/joys-challenges-rural-ministry/

- Concerns about the children's education

- The wife's career considerations

- Fear of adapting to a rural lifestyle

- Lack of pastoral training or experience

- Medical issues

- Wrong timing

- A perceived loss of professional status

- Limited access to decent coffee shops

- A belief that "I'm/we're just not cut out for country ministry"

While some of these reasons may be valid, others could be seen as misguided, easily combined, and weighed to justify whatever outcome appears most desirable in the given circumstances.

To paraphrase Isaiah 6: "Lord, here am I. Send someone else."

Transitioning to rural life and ministry requires a specific type of person. It is not for the faint-hearted and demands an honest realism when prayerfully considering the possibilities. Here are some important factors to consider:

1. Personal Suitability

- A clear sense of God's enabling for the task

- A willingness to form genuine connections with country people

- A strong marriage with a spouse who shares the call to rural ministry

- A healthy family unit

- A readiness to listen, learn, and embrace new ministry challenges

- A commitment to serve with limited external support

- A flexible and adaptable personality

- In some cases, a willingness to work bi-vocationally

2. Isolation Factors

- A readiness to live independently from extended family

- A willingness to cultivate meaningful new friendships within and outside the church community

- The need for a support network, whether locally or remotely, for spiritual and personal accountability and encouragement

3. Pastoral Considerations

- High turnover rates in some areas due to seasonal factors, drought, and economic fluctuations in farming and mining

- Stresses from economic and climatic challenges, leading to high unemployment, financial crises, and mental health issues

- The migration of young people to cities for higher education, with most not returning

- A shortage of gifted lay leaders

- Resistance to change in certain congregations

Rural ministry presents its own set of unique challenges, but it also offers rich rewards. While no pastor should assume a position with the expectation of earthly compensation, many rural pastors can attest to the special blessings and joys that stem from their ministries. These rewards may include:

1. Deep and Loyal Friendships

In rural settings, pastors and their families become beloved and respected members of the entire community, not just the local church. Engaging at various levels of community life, even simple activities like shopping, can transform into significant social events. Relationships develop easily and naturally, and by demonstrating a willingness to understand and embrace country life, barriers begin to dissolve.

2. Vast Ministry Experience

Country pastors are required to cultivate skills across multiple areas, including:

- Maintaining a weekly church program with a heavy preaching and teaching load

- Providing counseling and pastoral care in complex situations

- Conducting visitations in diverse rural settings

- Leading weddings and funerals for both the church and the broader community

- Organizing public events such as Easter, Christmas, Anzac Day, and school gatherings

- Engaging with community groups and networking with other clergy and churches in the area

3. Excellent Gospel Opportunities

Despite the secular nature of many small country towns, residents often maintain respect for churches and their Christian attendees. People may attend services sporadically or on special occasions, creating a greater openness to the gospel compared to urban areas. Personal conversations and hospitality flow more freely, and events like funerals can serve as invaluable opportunities to share the gospel as the community gathers. Pastors often enjoy a positive public image, leading community members to seek their guidance and advice.

4. The Rural Lifestyle

While some aspects of country living may seem challenging for those accustomed to the city's 'latte culture,' the appeal of life free from traffic, pollution, noise, and stress is undeniable. Although rural life is far from perfect, it offers a wholesome quality conducive to happy family life, productive ministry, and personal spiritual growth. Friendships are genuine, and people truly matter.

Considering these factors is crucial in rural ministry.

The urban ministry consists of congregations located in the inner cities and towns of today's world. This ministry holds a special place in my heart. In 2008, God led my family and me to Huntsville, AL, a city we had both vowed never to move to. Unbeknownst to me at the time, God had been preparing me for inner-city ministry since my youth. After facing many challenges and missed opportunities, God molded and shaped me for this calling. Once we became settled in our new surroundings, my wife and I embarked on our ministry journey. We were fortunate to serve in the inner city for over 13 years, where the joy we experienced far outweighed the challenges we faced.

5. The Essence of Ministry

[4]It didn't take long after the apostles' deaths for Christians to adopt some unusual ideas about ministry. Many people perceive ministry as a profession, often equating it with having a seminary degree. For most, ministry might involve activities such as serving

---

[4] DePra, David A., The Essence of True Ministry (The Good Nes – Home) https://www.goodnewsarticles.com/May05-2.htm

in a church, preaching sermons, or leading Bible studies. While these activities are certainly valuable—provided they are done biblically, they do not define the essence of ministry. That essence has never been about merely performing tasks.

Ministry is **"Life,"** His life. The best way to express it is this way: Christianity is **"Christ in us."** Our witness reflects **"Christ seen"** in us. However, our ministry is fundamentally about **"Christ working through us."**

The reality is that if my ministry isn't a result of His life operating first **"In me"** and then **"Through me,"** it cannot be considered His ministry. It may be **"My ministry,"** capable of achieving great things, large congregations, television ministries, and even the salvation of thousands. Yet, despite these impressive outcomes, if they stem from **"MY"** efforts rather than **"HIS,"** something essential will be absent. Tragically, we may not even realize it is missing.

Jesus always intended for His Body of believers to be living witnesses of Him, fueled by His life within them. True ministry emerges from this inner life, as demonstrated in the first century, which had a profound impact on the world. Unfortunately, it is often easier to engage in ministry and evangelism through the strength of religious flesh. This religious flesh can appear good and upright, and it demands far less than what is required to "BECOME" a genuine living witness.

If the church today could grasp this singular truth, everything would change. Once we recognize and embrace the true essence of ministry, the entire structure of professional ministry, financial systems, and much of what is practiced in churches will likely collapse. However, such a collapse would be beneficial, as it would pave the way for a community of believers who embody living witnesses of Jesus Christ and can be utilized by Him as ministers of His goals and purposes.

The essence of ministry is to embody and share the life of Christ. It transcends mere sermons or teachings; it is about the transformative impact of His life within us and through us to others. In essence, rather than treating ministry as a separate entity, we are called to "be" the ministry.

According to the Apostle Paul, the true cost of genuine ministry—the ministry of life to others—requires a form of death within ourselves. Many are reluctant to accept this necessity, yet it is crucial. Each of us carries aspects that can obstruct the flow and effectiveness of the Holy Spirit. For God to use us, we must allow these hindrances to die away.

It's important to recognize that ministry isn't simply a byproduct of reading books or acquiring knowledge. To "minister" involves far more than preaching and teaching, which, while valuable, are merely methods of delivery. The true essence of ministry lies in what God has accomplished in us through His Son. It is this inner transformation that God utilizes to impact the lives of others, aiming to edify and guide them toward maturity in Christ.

Therefore, seeing we have **this ministry**, as we have received mercy, we faint not; But have renounced the hidden things of dishonesty, not walking in craftiness, nor handling the word of God deceitfully; but by manifestation of the truth commending ourselves to every man's conscience in the sight of God. But if our gospel is hidden, it is hidden to those who are lost: In whom the god of this world hath blinded the minds of them which believe not, lest the light of the glorious gospel of Christ, who is the image of God, should shine unto them. For **we preach not ourselves**, but Christ Jesus the Lord; and ourselves your servants for Jesus' sake. For God, who commanded the light to shine out of darkness, hath shined in our hearts, to give the light of the knowledge of the glory of God in the face of Jesus Christ. But we have this treasure in earthen vessels, that the excellency of the power may be **of God**, and **not of us**. We are troubled on every side, yet not distressed; we are perplexed, but not in despair; Persecuted, but not forsaken; cast down, but not destroyed; Always bearing about in the body the dying of the Lord Jesus, that the life also of Jesus might be made manifest in our body. For we which live are always delivered unto death for Jesus' sake, that the life also of Jesus might be made manifest in our mortal flesh. 12 So then **death works in us, but life in you**. (2 Cor. 4:1-12 KJV)

6. Core Values and Principles

At the heart of ministry lies a commitment to core values such as compassion, service, integrity, and inclusivity. This section will explore how these values manifest in ministry practices and guide decision-making processes.

Compassion serves as the foundation of ministry. It drives individuals and organizations to empathize with the struggles and needs of others. In practice, this value manifests through outreach programs, counseling services, and community support initiatives that prioritize the well-being of those served. Decision-making processes are guided by a desire to understand and respond to the emotional and spiritual needs of individuals, ensuring that actions are taken with kindness and sensitivity.

Service is at the core of ministry, emphasizing a selfless dedication to helping others. This value is reflected in volunteer efforts, community development projects, and acts of kindness that aim to uplift those in need. In decision-making, the principle of service encourages leaders to prioritize the needs of others over personal or institutional gain. This commitment ensures that resources are allocated in ways that benefit the community, fostering a spirit of generosity and support.

Integrity is essential in maintaining trust and credibility in ministry practices. It involves being honest, ethical, and transparent in all dealings, both within the organization and with the community. This value manifests in clear communication, accountability, and adherence to ethical standards. Decision-making processes are guided by a commitment to doing what is right, even when it is challenging. Leaders are encouraged to model integrity, setting a tone that promotes ethical behavior throughout the ministry.

Inclusivity reflects a commitment to embracing diversity and ensuring that all individuals feel welcome and valued. This value is evident in efforts to reach out to marginalized communities, create safe spaces for dialogue, and engage in practices that promote equity. In decision-making, inclusivity encourages leaders to consider diverse perspectives and experiences, fostering an environment where everyone has a voice. This approach not only enriches ministry practices but also strengthens community bonds and promotes unity.

In summary, the core values of compassion, service, integrity, and inclusivity are integral to effective ministry. They shape how ministry is practiced and guide decision-making processes, ensuring that actions align with the mission of serving and uplifting others. By embodying these values, ministries can create a meaningful impact in their communities and foster a culture of love and respect.

7. Transformational Impact

Ministry has the potential to transform lives and communities. By examining case studies of effective ministries, this section will highlight the tangible outcomes of ministry efforts, including social change, personal development, and community cohesion.

"Transformation impact in ministry" refers to the profound, lasting change a ministry has on individuals and communities, where people experience a significant shift in their lives, values, and behaviors, often attributed to their engagement with the ministry's teachings, programs, and outreach efforts, moving them closer to their spiritual goals or addressing critical life issues.

Key aspects of transformation impact in ministry:

- **Personal growth:**

Individuals experience personal development in areas like character, faith, and decision-making due to the ministry's influence. A strong character builds trust and respect among peers and the community. When leaders demonstrate integrity, humility, and compassion, they become role models. People are more likely to follow and be influenced by someone whose actions consistently align with their values.

Deepening one's faith can provide clarity, purpose, and resilience. A strong personal faith can inspire others, as individuals often look to leaders for spiritual guidance. A mature faith also equips leaders to navigate challenges with grace, demonstrating reliance on their beliefs, which can encourage others to deepen their own faith.

Effective decision-making is crucial in ministry. Growth in this area involves making wise choices and considering the impact of those choices on the community. Leaders who are adept at decision-making can effectively address challenges and seize opportunities, which can lead to positive change and inspire others to engage actively in ministry.

Personal growth in these areas often leads to a more authentic and relatable ministry. When leaders exhibit growth, it invites others to pursue their own development, fostering a culture where personal transformation is valued and encouraged.

Strong character and sound decision-making facilitate healthier relationships within the community. When individuals feel valued and understood, they are more likely to engage and contribute, amplifying the ministry's reach and impact. Therefore, personal growth in character, faith, and decision-making creates a foundation for effective ministry influence, as it cultivates trust, inspires others, and fosters a supportive community.

- **Spiritual renewal:**

A deepened connection with God leads to a more meaningful spiritual life. Spiritual renewal often involves a fresh encounter with God, reigniting passion, and commitment to one's faith. This renewed enthusiasm can lead to a more vibrant prayer life, increased worship, and a deeper engagement with scripture.

Through spiritual renewal, individuals often gain clearer insights into their purpose and calling. This clarity can foster a stronger sense of direction in life, aligning personal goals with spiritual values, which enhances the meaning of daily activities. Renewal typically involves a process of introspection and transformation. As individuals reflect on their beliefs and behaviors, they may experience significant changes in their attitudes and priorities, leading to a more authentic relationship with God.

Spiritual renewal can encourage individuals to seek community and fellowship with others who share similar values. Engaging in a supportive spiritual community can provide encouragement, accountability, and opportunities for collective worship, deepening connections with God and others. Regular experiences of renewal can increase awareness of God's presence in everyday life. This heightened sensitivity can lead to a more profound appreciation for the divine in both mundane and extraordinary moments, enriching the spiritual journey.

A renewed spirit often compels individuals to serve others, reflecting God's love and grace. This service can deepen one's connection to God by embodying His teachings and fostering a sense of fulfillment and purpose.

Spiritual renewal facilitates a deeper connection with God by revitalizing faith, clarifying purpose, transforming the heart, fostering community, increasing awareness, and inspiring service. These elements collectively contribute to a more meaningful and enriched spiritual life.

- **Community transformation:**

The ministry positively impacts the wider community by addressing social issues, fostering unity, and encouraging positive change. Community transformation initiatives often focus on identifying and tackling pressing social issues such as poverty, education, health care, and housing. By mobilizing resources and engaging community members, these initiatives can create targeted programs that provide support, raise awareness, and implement solutions, ultimately improving the quality of life for residents.

Transformation efforts can bring diverse groups together, promoting collaboration and understanding among different demographics. By working towards common goals, communities can break down barriers, reduce divisions, and foster a sense of belonging and solidarity, leading to stronger, more cohesive neighborhoods. As communities engage in transformation, they often inspire individuals to become more active participants in their environment. This can lead to increased volunteerism, civic engagement, and advocacy for local issues. When residents feel empowered to effect change, it creates a culture of responsibility and initiative that can have lasting effects on the community.

Community transformation fosters resilience by equipping individuals and groups with the skills, resources, and networks needed to navigate challenges. This resilience can help communities better respond to crises, adapt to change, and sustain progress over time. Many transformation initiatives focus on economic development, creating jobs, and supporting local businesses. By enhancing economic opportunities, communities can reduce poverty and improve overall well-being, which positively impacts the wider community. When successful transformation occurs, it can instill a sense of hope and possibility among community members. This hopeful outlook can motivate individuals to aspire for better futures, pursue education, and engage in positive behaviors that contribute to the overall health and vitality of the community.

- **Holistic approach:**

Transformation goes beyond just spiritual aspects, encompassing emotional, mental, and physical well-being. It involves understanding and processing emotions. A holistic approach encourages emotional intelligence, helping individuals identify and express their feelings. Tools such as therapy, journaling, and mindfulness practices can facilitate emotional healing and resilience, allowing for healthier relationships and improved self-acceptance. Your mental health is crucial for your overall well-being. Holistic transformation promotes cognitive health through practices such as meditation, cognitive-behavioral therapy, and stress management techniques. It emphasizes the importance of a positive mindset, lifelong learning, and mental stimulation, which collectively enhance clarity, focus, and creativity.

The physical aspect focuses on nurturing the body through nutrition, exercise, and sleep. A complete approach advocates for a balanced diet, regular physical activity, and adequate rest, recognizing that physical health directly impacts emotional and mental states. Integrative practices like yoga and exercise can also harmonize body and mind. This universal model understands that these aspects are consistent. For instance, poor physical health can lead to emotional distress, while mental challenges can affect physical health. By addressing all dimensions together, individuals can achieve a more robust and lasting transformation.

Holistic transformation encourages self-awareness and personal growth through various practices like self-reflection, goal setting, and community involvement. This growth fosters a sense of purpose and fulfillment, further enhancing overall well-being. Please consider the interplay between spiritual, emotional, mental, and physical dimensions. A holistic approach fosters a more comprehensive and sustainable transformation, leading to a healthier, more balanced life.

- **Discipleship programs:**

Intentional mentoring and teaching to help individuals grow in their faith and apply biblical principles to daily life is key. Intentional mentoring allows for tailored guidance based on the unique needs, experiences, and spiritual maturity of individuals. Mentors can address specific challenges and questions, providing relevant biblical insights. These Mentors who live out their faith serve as living examples of biblical principles. This modeling helps mentees see how to embody these principles in various aspects of life, encouraging them to follow suit.

Also, we have discipleship programs that foster deep relationships between mentors and mentees. These relationships create a safe environment for unprotected discussions about faith, struggles, and personal growth, leading to deeper understanding and commitment. Maintaining regular check-ins and discussions in mentoring relationships promotes accountability. This encourages individuals to stay committed to their spiritual goals and apply biblical teachings consistently. Accountability is crucial in all aspects of life, but especially in your ministry.

We must be intentional through our teaching, which often involves studying scripture together and helping individuals learn how to interpret and apply biblical texts to their daily lives. This direct engagement with the Word strengthens their understanding and application of faith. Therefore, individuals can be encouraged to serve in their communities, applying their faith in action. This not only enhances personal growth but also fosters a sense of belonging within the church and broader community. This can introduce and encourage the practice of spiritual disciplines like prayer, fasting, and meditation, helping individuals cultivate a deeper relationship with God and a more robust faith life. It can also facilitate discussions of real-life situations and challenges. Mentors can help mentees navigate how to apply biblical principles in practical ways, making faith relevant to their everyday experiences.

- **Small group ministry:**

Creating intimate environments for sharing, support, and accountability among ministry members and the community. In this ministry, it is essential to establish clear ground rules that promote confidentiality and respect. This encourages members to share their thoughts and feelings without fear of judgment. When a person feels they will be judged, they are more unlikely to share their feelings. The ministry leader should motivate members to attend regular meetings to develop trust among members. He or she should engage in activities that promote fellowship, such as group outings or shared meals, which can strengthen bonds.

The small group ministry needs to Implement guided sharing sessions where members can discuss personal experiences and struggles. This can be facilitated through reminders or questions that encourage open and honest communication, promoting vulnerability. The need for individuals to open up and share is there. The ministry leader prerequisites to make the members feel heard through teaching and practicing active listening skills. He or she can incorporate prayer into meetings, allowing members to pray for each other's specific needs. This spiritual connection can deepen relationships and provide support. Through relationship building, members can form accountability partnerships, checking each other's progress toward goals and growth, which fosters a sense of responsibility. Displaying and Highlighting an individual's strengths and progress can and will build confidence and a sense of community.

The small group can nurture and provide training on effective communication and conflict resolution. The group may offer resources that can equip group members with tools to support one another. This will lead to creating opportunities for members to give and receive feedback about the group's dynamics, adopting a culture of continuous improvement and openness.

- **Outreach initiatives:**

Generates you to actively engage with people in need within the community, offering practical assistance and spiritual guidance. This begins by shepherding assessments or focus groups to identify the specific needs of the community. Understanding the challenges people face will help tailor your outreach efforts effectively. We need to learn to collaborate with local organizations, businesses, and government agencies that share a similar mission. This can amplify resources and reach more individuals in need. It will also produce opportunities for church members to volunteer in outreach programs, which is important. This not only aids those in need but also cultivates a sense of community and involvement among members.

Organize events such as food drives, health fairs, or clothing distribution days. These events can serve as practical assistance while providing a platform for spiritual conversations and support. In addition, establish support groups for various issues such as addiction, grief, or financial struggles. These groups can provide emotional and spiritual support, creating a safe space for individuals to share their experiences. These needs will always exist; it's a matter of meeting them. In the process, offer counseling or mentorship programs that provide individuals with spiritual guidance and practical advice. This can happen in person, over the phone, or even virtually. In the past, there were fewer outlets, but now the door is wide open. For more opportunities, consider hosting workshops on topics such as budgeting, job seeking, parenting, or mental health. Providing education empowers individuals and offers a chance for spiritual mentorship.

Occasions always exist for volunteers to go into neighborhoods to engage with residents, offer help, and share about the ministry's resources. This can be a way to build relationships and trust within the community. It will form opportunities for prayer, which can be through several avenues. In today's society, it may be accomplished through organized prayer walks, prayer chains, or simply inviting community members to share their prayer requests. But please follow up on all requests. After this initial outreach effort, ensure there is a system in place to follow up with those who received assistance as well. This can help build ongoing relationships and provide continued support. By integrating these strategies, the ministry can create a meaningful impact in the lives of individuals while promoting a sense of community involvement and spiritual growth.

- **Leadership development:**

Equip individuals with skills to become leaders within the church and community. This can be done by pairing emerging leaders with experienced leaders within the ministry. This one-on-one relationship can provide guidance, support, and practical insights into leadership roles. Then organize workshops focusing on various leadership skills such as communication, conflict resolution, team building, and strategic planning. Tailor these workshops to address specific challenges faced in your ministry. You may also implement structured discipleship initiatives that not only focus on spiritual growth but also include leadership training. This can help those in the ministry develop a greater understanding of their faith while cultivating leadership qualities.

Make sure to encourage members to take on leadership roles in service projects or ministry activities. Trust me, there will be some who oppose it is the ministry leader's duty to persuade everyone to engage and participate. Remember, real-life experience is invaluable for developing confidence and practical skills. Try to create an ethnicity of feedback where leaders can receive constructive criticism and encouragement. This helps to grow their skills and advances their accountability. In doing so, you want to organize retreats that focus on spiritual renewal and leadership development. These retreats can provide a space for reflection, prayer, and strategic thinking about the ministry's direction.

You will need leaders to be involved in the vision-setting process of the ministry. Allowing them to contribute to the ministry's mission can instill a sense of ownership and commitment. This will encourage participation from a diverse range of individuals in various leadership capacities, such as teaching, organizing events, or leading small groups. This multiplicity can enrich the ministry and foster inclusive leadership. At the same time, promoting a society of lifelong learning by providing access to books, online courses, and seminars on leadership and ministry-related topics. This can motivate leaders to continually grow and adapt. Lastly, in leadership development, identify and celebrate the accomplishments of leaders within the ministry. This not only encourages those individuals but also motivates others to step into leadership roles.

8. Challenges in Ministry

[5]Despite its noble purpose, the ministry faces various challenges, including burnout, societal changes, and the need for cultural competency. This section will discuss these challenges and offer

---

[5] Fields, Doug, your first two years in youth ministry (Grands Rapids: Zondervan, 2002) pgs. 41-49

strategies for resilience and adaptation in the face of evolving community needs.

Discouragement can indeed be a formidable barrier, often leading to feelings of isolation and hopelessness among leaders. Acknowledging this reality is the first step toward resilience. It's essential for ministry leaders to create an environment where vulnerability is welcomed, allowing for open discussions about struggles and discouragement. Building a supportive community can help dispel the loneliness that often accompanies leadership roles.

Focusing on the core purpose of ministry—serving God and others—can also provide clarity and motivation during tough times. Encouraging leaders to seek guidance through prayer, mentorship, and fellowship can foster a sense of renewal and strength. Ultimately, recognizing that discouragement is a common experience can help leaders navigate their challenges with grace and perseverance, leading to a more fulfilling and long-lasting ministry.

Ministry can cause burnout very easily. The focus has to remain on God, and the body must get its rest. Trying to be everything to everyone and trying to be everywhere at once will never work. Trust God and his process and be what you can but also recognize what you can't. Learn how to adapt to situations and also learn what's beyond your control. There will be those who show disrespect, lack trust, are not dependable, etc., but know if God calls you to ministry, he will see you through the ministry. Never carry useless weight; that is not called for.

A strong prayer life is essential for anyone in ministry. Allow the Holy Spirit to guide and inspire you as you serve. Do not underestimate the power of the Holy Spirit; instead, let Him lead you. Prayer enables God to take control while you submit to His will. Never fall into the trap of thinking that you know ministry so well that prayer becomes an afterthought. For a ministry to thrive spiritually, it must glorify God and uplift the name of Jesus. Only God knows the direction He wants His ministry to take, so seek His wisdom in all matters.

After dedicating time to prayer, observe how your ministry unfolds and develops. God will always provide opportunities for you to minister to others. Throughout my ministry, I have faced numerous challenges and joys, but one of the most memorable experiences occurred recently. A youth minister who had served with me years ago reached out to me. This was significant because, at the time of our service together, his wife was the director of our learning center while he served as youth minister. During their tenure, after much prayer, a difficult decision was made to terminate her position, which created a significant rift between the husband, the youth minister, and me. Shortly after, he resigned. His resignation caused great turbulence in the church, the youth department, and the learning center.

I will never forget our last conversation, as it brought devastation not only to their lives but also to my ministry. Being young and inexperienced, I made a hasty decision that nearly jeopardized my work. However, recently, that same youth minister, now serving as an assistant minister at another congregation, called me. His call brought tears to my eyes. To my surprise, he congratulated me on the growth and success of my ministry and offered words of encouragement. Before we ended our conversation, we both recognized that God had allowed our paths to cross in order to guide us to where He intended us to be. Now, both of us are thriving, and God continues to enable us to flourish in ministry. I am thankful for the time the Lord allowed us to spend and serve in a capacity of humility.

The art and essence of ministry entails the young and the old. [6]In the book "Sticky Faith," Dr. Kara E. Powell and Dr. Chap Clark discuss how college students are influenced by various aspects of ministry, emphasizing the importance of developing a faith that lasts beyond adolescence. They highlight several key points regarding the art and essence of ministry in relation to college students.

The book emphasizes the importance of forming genuine relationships within ministry settings. College students thrive in environments where they feel connected and valued. Mentorship and community support play a crucial role in helping them navigate their faith during this transitional period. Many students are faced with the inducement of sex, drugs, and alcohol. This can and will cause students to lose their faith and even experience a lack of trust in God. That's why it's vital to implement ministries that foster student engagement in service to the ministry. By participating in service and outreach, it helps college students see the practical application of their faith. Engaging in ministry allows them to develop a sense of purpose and identity, reinforcing their beliefs through action.

The book "Sticky Faith" emphasizes that college students benefit from opportunities to engage with their faith in both their academic and social lives. Therefore, we need ministries that encourage students to explore how their beliefs intersect with various aspects of life to promote a deeper, more robust faith. The book continues to advocate creating a safe space for students to ask questions and express doubts. Ministries that welcome assessment and discussion about faith can help students develop a more vigorous understanding of their faith.

---

[6] Powell, Dr. Kara E. and Clark, Dr. Chap, sticky faith (Grand Rapids: Zondervan, 2011) pgs. 17-20

The role of family and community in shaping faith is emphasized. Often, college students who maintain connections with their faith communities feel a stronger sense of belonging and continuity in their spiritual journeys. Students need to remain connected to ministry while balancing school, church, work, faith, and family. By focusing on these elements, Powell and Clark demonstrate that the art and essence of ministry can have a profound impact on college students, helping them cultivate a "sticky faith" that endures beyond their college years.

[7]There are other avenues of ministry to consider. Dr. Luis R. Lugo discusses in his book, "The Five-Fold Work of the Evangelist: God's Church Administrator," how the minister and the evangelist work in ministry. The primary task of the evangelist is to preach the word, the gospel of Jesus Christ. His primary obligation is to make a proclamation of the death, burial, and resurrection of Jesus Christ for the remission of sins (1 Cor. 15:1-4). As Dr. Lugo states, and I quote, "preaching is the avenue by which the power of God is transmitted to those who are in sin and in need of restoration, rejuvenation, reconciliation, and reconstruction (1 Cor. 1:21)." His message is to give hope to the hopeless, sight to the blind, strength to the weak, and give help to the helpless. The evangelist is a herald for God, and the message is from God (1 Peter 4:15). For the man of God, the evangelist, to be effective, he must spend time in study (2 Tim. 2:15), meditation (Ps. 1), prayer (Acts 6:4), and have contact with the people (1 Tim. 4:12-16).

The evangelist's ministry includes equipping the church for maturity, enabling them to carry out the work of ministry and help build up the body of Christ. He is responsible for teaching the church to be objective and persistent in personal study and to be honest and diligent in searching the Scriptures. He must understand that not everyone will agree with his interpretation of God's word,

---

[7] Lugo, Luis R, M.Th, The Five Fold Work of the Evangelist: God's Church Administrator (Columbus: Brentwood Christian Press, 1995)

often due to their own lack of study and understanding. His duties include admonishing the disorderly, caring for the faint-hearted, supporting the weak, being patient, and promoting love over retaliation. He is also accountable for training elders, deacons, teachers, and the church.

As he navigates through his ministry, he will set things in order. The question is, what are the things that he is responsible for setting in order? He is to set in order the worship of the New Testament church, evangelism and missions, benevolence, discipline, and governmental structure. This is important that he keeps the church sound in doctrine and in faith. Christ has ordained New Testament worship, and the evangelist is held accountable by Christ to implement what Jesus established. This tells how to sing, pray, communion, give, and the act of preaching.

Another ministry and work of the evangelist is defending the faith. In the book of 2 Timothy 1:13-14, Paul says, “Hold fast the form of sound words, which thou have heard of me, in faith and love which is Jesus Christ. That good thing which was committed unto thee keep by the Holy Spirit which dwelleth in us.” Before the man of God can defend the faith, his attitude his faith must be what God has ordained of those he seeks to correct! Notice it was obvious that the church at Ephesus was being attacked with some type of false teaching. Paul instructs the man of God to hold fast the word against these heresies.

The evangelist's calling is to preach everywhere, to everyone, and every word that proceeds out of the mouth of God. Paul mentions in the book of Acts 20 and verse 20 that he had taught them “publicly” and “from house to house.” Whether in masse or one-on-one, Paul communicated the gospel in every atmosphere of life. He preached “both to the Jews and also to the Greeks.” Paul was burdened for the Jews and called to the Gentiles but loved the lost, of every color and race. There’s an inherent impartiality to the evangelist calling.

He doesn't simply preach to those like us but to all. Paul "kept back nothing..." and preached "repentance toward God and faith toward our Lord Jesus Christ" and let it be known that he had "not shunned to declare unto you all the counsel of God." In other words, Paul covered the bases and shared everything God wanted him to share. He introduced every subject and avoided nothing. There was a threat upon his life and ministry, but he refused to be swayed in the least. He wouldn't be moved!

[8]Dr. Kerry Williams, a distinguished teacher and expositor of the Word, provides valuable guidance for evangelists aiming to establish a successful ministry. His book is specifically designed for ministers, addressing the unique challenges and responsibilities of their work within the kingdom.

Dr. Williams emphasizes that ministry is unlike any other profession. While it presents its own set of difficulties, it also requires a distinct skill set. The role of a minister resembles that of a shepherd; even if one is not an elder, one must listen to the complaints, suggestions, and celebrations of their parishioners. However, it's important to acknowledge that ministry can lead to burnout if one is not careful. Many ministers have stepped away from their calling for various reasons, making it essential for them to be equipped to navigate the ups and downs of ministry life.

The book offers numerous strategies to support ministers in their endeavors, but one crucial takeaway is found on page 15: a minister must be aware of where they are leading their congregation and where God is guiding them. To achieve this, setting goals is imperative. These goals should include both short-term and long-term objectives. Working towards these goals enables ministers to realize their dreams.

---

[8] Williams, Kerry W, PhD, An Able Spokesman: Tips for Building an Effective Ministry (Columbia: USA, 2024) pgs. 3, 15

Long-term goals serve as foundational pillars necessary for ministry to flourish and become a reality. In contrast, short-term goals focus on building the groundwork for these long-term aspirations. Ministers must learn to dream big for their ministries and actively pursue those dreams to bring them to fruition.

As I respectfully conclude my reflections on the duties and calling of the evangelist, I would like to outline three key designations pertaining to the title of a man of God. In the New Testament, there are three terms that describe God's worker known as a preacher. These terms not only characterize the individual but also highlight the responsibilities that God expects of him. The three terms are minister, preacher, and evangelist.

1. **Minister** (Greek: *diakonos*)

The term "minister" refers to one who serves—a servant. A preacher is fundamentally a minister or servant of Jesus Christ, as seen in 1 Timothy 4:6. His role is to serve the Lord's Word and proclaim the Gospel to all people (Acts 6:4; Romans 15:16). A "good minister of Jesus Christ" is called to "put the brethren in remembrance of these things" (1 Timothy 4:6). Furthermore, he must "take heed to the ministry which he has received in the Lord, that he fulfill it" (Colossians 4:17).

2. **Preacher** (Greek: *kerux*)

The term "preacher" signifies a herald—a public proclaimer who authoritatively declares the king's law to the people, which must be obeyed. The Lord has authorized (1 Timothy 2:7; 2 Timothy 1:11) and sent out His preachers or "heralds" to spread His message throughout the world (Romans 10:14-18). Their primary duty is to proclaim His message, the Gospel (2 Timothy 2:1-7; 4:1-5), and they are called to share only His message (Romans 10:15; 15:19; Galatians 1:6-10; 1 Thessalonians 2:9).

3. **Evangelist** (Greek: *euangelistes*)

An "evangelist" is characterized as a messenger of good news. Christ has given evangelists (Ephesians 4:11-12) the responsibility to deliver His message, the "gospel," which translates to "good news." Paul cautioned preachers to "do the work of an evangelist, make full proof of thy ministry" (1 Timothy 4:5). A preacher is instructed to "preach the word; be instant in season, out of season; reprove, rebuke, exhort with all longsuffering and doctrine" (2 Timothy 4:2).

Much of the misunderstanding surrounding preachers and their roles stems from an incorrect perception of the relationship between the preacher and the local church. Many people view the preacher as an employee of the church, leading to the belief that the church, as the employer, dictates the scope and responsibilities of his work. This perspective is often summarized in the phrase, "We pay the preacher, so we tell him what to do."

However, the Lord's instruction to compensate preachers for their preaching (1 Cor. 9:14) does not categorize them as church employees. This support is likened to that of God's priests (1 Cor. 9:13-14), who were sustained by the offerings of the people presented to the Lord, serving as His ministers rather than as mere hirelings (Num. 18:1-20).

A preacher should not be viewed as an employee of any church but rather as a servant of the Lord (1 Tim. 4:6). He is ultimately accountable to God, tasked with fulfilling the Lord's work, and is cautioned against becoming entangled in worldly affairs so that he may please the One who has chosen him to be a soldier (2 Tim. 2:3-4).

The biblical relationship between a preacher and the members who support him is one of fellow workers in the service of the Lord. The Lord instructs the preacher to share the gospel, while those who listen are called to provide support for his mission. Together, they share in "fellowship in the gospel" (1 Cor. 9:6-14; Phil. 1:5-7).

One of the most imperative, if not the most significant, in the church is the children/youth ministry. This ministry allows the congregation to exist in the future. Without children, there's no future.

Youth ministry is crucial to church growth by cultivating the next generation of leaders and engaged members. It advances a sense of belonging and commitment while promoting spiritual development, resulting in a stronger, more vibrant congregation. The involvement of youth in church is essential, as young members often encourage their parents to attend services and motivate their peers to join the youth group. Additionally, they act as ambassadors for the church within the community, contributing to fulfilling the mission and the congregation's growth.

Although the contributions of elders are significant as leaders, achieving sustainable long-term growth depends on the active participation of young people. The modern church must focus on furthering the spiritual growth of the youth to equip them for meaningful engagement in church activities and programs. Youth ministry initiatives are vital in supporting young individuals' social, spiritual, and emotional development, helping them become leaders and role models for their peers.

Training and developing young people require time, which can lead to a decline in their participation in church activities. Therefore, investing in those who are present empowers and equips them to become young disciples. Church leaders can use this knowledge to recognize the importance of promoting programs that reach a broader audience and enhance spiritual growth. Additionally, leaders should view young people as current leaders by assigning them manageable tasks, highlighting their improvement within the Church.

Investing in today's youth is necessary for growing the body of Christ. Teaching young people in the church to grow in their relationship with the Lord can prepare them to serve Christ in all they do. As a result, this nurtures the congregation and allows the church to flourish.

Serving young people prepares them to become future leaders and allows them to contribute to the church. This is seen many times in the Bible, as God often utilized young people to do great things. For example, God used Timothy to minister and lead the Ephesian church when he was young.

In addition, there is much to be learned from the faith of a child. Matthew 18:2-4 says, "He called a little child to him, and placed the child among them. And he said: 'Truly I tell you, unless you change and become like little children, you will never enter the kingdom of heaven. Therefore, whoever takes the lowly position of this child is the greatest in the kingdom of heaven.'" Because of God's heart for young people, it is important to recognize their value in today's church.

A key challenge for many churches is how to design youth programs that break down barriers and encourage genuine engagement, spiritual growth, and personal development for participants from various backgrounds. The differences between youth and their elders can impact their willingness to engage in church life. The church outreach programs and community engagement initiatives aimed at young people are designed to foster growth and address their unique needs as a vital demographic for leading others to salvation. Youth ministry activities focus on nurturing spiritual development, sharing religious teachings, offering mentorship, building a sense of peer community, promoting positive youth development, and strengthening lasting connections between young people and the church.

[9]Andrew Root's book The End of Youth Ministry is very stimulating. While it offers insights from a parent's perspective, it also explores many other areas. In chapter two, Root shares the story of a young man named Graham. Understanding Graham's mindset and how he views youth ministry is intriguing. He sees youth ministry as a way to help young people avoid wasting their lives. This perspective holds truth—by staying engaged and active, they can spend their time meaningfully. However, Graham then asks Andrew, "What do you think youth ministry is for?"

His answer was simply God. When we think about other creatures or animals, they seem to always make something out of nothing, but we humans will waste our time with any and everything.

My two sons mean the world to me, and as my oldest prepares to head off to college on a football scholarship, I find myself wrestling with a philosophical concern. It's not his education, safety, or even the distance that troubles me most; it's the fear of him drifting away from his faith. I want to ensure that wherever he chooses to go, the local church congregation will keep him engaged and connected to God.

I have been praying that the school he selects will lead him closer to God rather than away from Him. My heart longs for him to maintain his faith while benefiting from a free education. After much prayer, it became clear that God had other plans; out of six scholarship offers, only two remained open. Unfortunately, the university my son, my wife, and I hoped he would attend was not among them. I had my heart set on an out-of-state university, while my wife preferred one closer to home.

---

[9] Root, Andrew, The End of Youth Ministry? (Grand Rapids: Baker Academic, 2020) pgs. 5,6

The options left were Arizona Christian University in Glendale, AZ, and Tennessee Valley in Huntsville, AL, our hometown. While my wife felt at peace with the situation, I struggled, so I began to pray for him to find a church with a vibrant youth ministry nearby where he could get involved.

In a beautiful turn of events, the Lord opened a door that we thought was closed. My son ultimately signed with Bethel University in McKenzie, TN, which is just a short 3-hour drive from home. He will be attending a church of Christ with an active youth ministry, allowing him to engage and contribute meaningfully. We are all thrilled with this outcome. Ironically, Bethel University was his first choice.

Youth need guidance and support as they navigate through the most challenging part of their development and seek to grow in their walk with Christ. Christ-like leaders are needed to serve young members of the congregation and help them to reach their full potential.

[10]As we embark on this journey in youth ministry, it's essential to examine the teenage brain and its significance in youth ministry work. Mark Oestreicher's book, "Parent's Guide to Understanding Teenage Brains: Why They Act the Way They Do," offers valuable insights into this topic. To create an impactful youth ministry, we must understand the daily challenges young people face.

The book addresses the most significant changes occurring in teenagers, beginning with the physical transformations that parents and youth ministers often notice first. These changes, whether related to sexual development, body shape, or voice, are evident externally before the internal shifts become obvious. While these physical changes are significant and should not be underestimated,

---

[10] Oestreicher, Mark, A Parent's Guide to Understanding Teenage Brains: Why They Act the Way They Do (simplyyouthministry.com: 2012) pgs. 6-10.

they are also accompanied by deeper emotional and cognitive changes that teenagers are navigating.

Many teenagers are preoccupied with their physical appearance but are also acutely aware of the complex changes taking place in their lives. This often leads to moments of self-doubt, where they question if they are "turning out wrong." Consequently, the most significant change during adolescence occurs within their brains. While this transformation can be difficult for parents to recognize, a supportive youth ministry fosters an environment where teens feel safe to be open and honest. Such an approach nurtures their growth and maturity as they transition into adulthood. Therefore, understanding the teenage brain is essential, as it operates distinctly differently from an adult brain and should be approached with that awareness.

[11]Effective ministry requires strong leaders to guide the way. In Michael Hyatt's book, "The Vision Driven Leader," he shares a quote from Beau Lotto: "What defines a good leader? Enabling other people to step into the unseen." Additionally, leaders should heed John F. Kennedy's words: "Those who look only to the past or present are certain to miss the future." This book is filled with insights on the necessity of visionary leadership in ministry. An effective ministry thrives under a leader who is people-oriented, patient and committed to bringing out the best in others. Ministries should not remain static; as communities evolve and needs change, so too must the ministry. Many ministries struggle due to a lack of effective leadership. Leaders must recognize when a ministry has fulfilled its purpose or identify new ministries that are needed within a particular community.

Lastly, as we examine the art and essence of ministry, we must include how technology influences modern ministry practices.

---

[11] Hyatt, Michael, The Vision Driven Leader (Grand Rapids: Baker Books Publishing, 2020)

There are 12 things to consider in modern-day technology and ministry:

1. Improved Communication: Technology facilitates instant communication through emails, social media, and messaging apps, allowing ministries to share updates, events, and messages effectively.

2. Online Worship Services: Streaming services and virtual gatherings enable ministries to reach a broader audience, allowing people to participate in worship from anywhere, which is especially valuable for those unable to attend in person.

3. Digital Resources: Ministries can provide access to a wealth of online resources, such as sermons, Bible studies, and educational materials, making it easier for members to engage with content at their convenience.

4. Social Media Engagement: Platforms like Facebook, Instagram, and Twitter enable ministries to connect with members and potential visitors, share inspirational content, and foster community engagement.

5. Virtual Community Building: Online forums and groups allow members to connect, share experiences, and support one another, creating a sense of community that extends beyond physical gatherings.

6. Data Management: Technology helps ministries manage member information, track attendance, and analyze engagement through database systems and church management software, improving organizational efficiency.

7. Online Giving: Digital payment solutions make it easier for members to contribute financially, offering options for one-time donations or recurring giving through websites or mobile apps.

8. Educational Opportunities: Online courses and webinars provide opportunities for spiritual growth and leadership training, making learning accessible to a wider audience.

9. Outreach and Evangelism: Ministries can utilize digital marketing strategies to reach new audiences, advertise events, and share their mission beyond their immediate geographical area.

10. Content Creation: Technology allows for the creation of diverse content, including podcasts, blogs, and videos, which can be shared widely and resonate with different demographics.

11. Virtual Events: Hosting events online, such as conferences or retreats, makes participation more accessible and can attract people from various locations.

12. Accessibility: Technology can enhance accessibility for individuals with disabilities or those who may have difficulty attending in person, ensuring that everyone can participate in ministry activities.

By leveraging technology, ministries can enhance their effectiveness, broaden their reach, and create more meaningful connections within their communities. However, it's essential to balance technology use with personal interactions to maintain the relational aspect of ministry.

Conclusion

The art and essence of ministry are formulated through Jesus. Jesus is the ultimate example of the art and ministry at its best. In Ken Blanchard & Phil Hodges's book, "Lead Like Jesus," numerous examples and information are given for effective ministry. This world is seeking a different leadership role model than that of tradition. Popular opinion has created a leadership model, but there is a better way. Jesus is the Great I Am, and His Way is the only way. Ministry leaders must exemplify Christlike characteristics. To be your best in your ministry, you must demonstrate Jesus in your life as well as in your ministry. The question is, how do I lead like Jesus to have an effective ministry? A leader is considered one who influences others. In ministry, you must be able to influence others. Leaders are not men or women just with a title, but those who have a servant's heart in a life role relationship. Jesus fed over 5000, healed the sick, caused the blind to see and the lame to walk, brought life to the dead and did much more in His ministry. Therefore, the ministry gives the opportunity to help others with health, finances, food, transportation, housing, etc., to lead a person to Jesus.

People often seek improvement from external sources, but to lead like Jesus, the transformation must begin internally. When a person's heart is changed, the outward expression will naturally follow. As noted, "The most persistent barrier to leading like Jesus is a heart motivated by self-interest." In Philippians 2:1-4, the Apostle Paul emphasizes the importance of prioritizing the interests of others over our own. A heart driven by self-interest tends to prioritize receiving over giving, placing personal agendas, safety, recognition, and gratification above the needs of others. In contrast, a servant leader focuses on serving others and respects the desires of those who have entrusted them with influence and responsibility. Meanwhile, a self-serving leader believes they should lead while others simply follow. That's why it's important to lead like Jesus in your ministry, so your ministry will be fulfilling to Christ and his kingdom.

The art and essence of ministry are deeply connected, showcasing a vibrant relationship between creative expression and core values. As society evolves, the practice of ministry must adapt to address the diverse needs of various communities, all while remaining anchored in its fundamental mission of service and transformation.

Biography

1. Bales, Dr. James D. *The Deacon & His Work*. Lubbock: Sunset Institute Press, 1986

2. Blanchard, Ken and Hodges, Phil. *Lead Like Jesus*. Nashville: Thomas Nelson, 2005.

3. Fields, Doug. *Your First Two Years in Youth Ministry: A Personal and Practical Guide to Starting Right*. Grand Rapids: Zondervan, 2002.

4. Gilman, John. *7 Steps to Launching a Successful Ministry*. ACS Technologies, 2022. https://www.acstechnologies.com/church-growth/7-steps-launching-successful-ministry

5. Lugo M.Th., Luis R. *The Five Fold Work of the Evangelist*. Columbus: Brentwood Christian Press, 1995

6. Oestreicher, Mark. *A Parent's Guide to Understanding Teenage Brains: Why They Act the Way They DO*. USA: Group.com, 2012.

7. Powell, Dr. Kara E., and Clark, Dr. Chap. *Sticky Faith*. Grand Rapids: Zondervan, 2011.

8. Root, Andrew. *The End of Youth Ministry*. Grand Rapids: Baker Academic, 2020.

9. Shabazz, Dr. O.J. *Excellence in Ministry: A Guide to Protocols and Etiquette for Church Leaders*. Orlando: 2023.

10. Williams PhD, Kerry W. *An Able Spokesman: Tips for Building an Effective Ministry*. Columbia: 2023.

Made in the USA
Columbia, SC
02 June 2025